SAFE AND SOUND

Handbook for Personal Safety and Self-Defense

HARIKUMAR V T

PREFACE

Welcome to "Safe and Sound: Handbook for Personal Safety and Self-Defense." This book is a comprehensive guide designed to empower you with the knowledge and skills necessary to navigate the complexities of personal safety and self-defense in today's world. Whether you are a complete beginner or have some experience in this domain, this handbook is tailored to meet your needs and equip you with practical strategies to enhance your safety and well-being.

In recent years, concerns about personal safety have become increasingly prevalent. From news reports of assaults and robberies to the rise of cyber threats and scams, it is evident that individuals must be proactive in safeguarding themselves and their loved ones. However, the topic of personal safety and self-defense can be overwhelming and intimidating, often leaving people unsure of where to start or how to protect themselves effectively.

This is where "Safe and Sound" comes in. Our goal with this handbook is to demystify personal safety and self-defense, providing you with clear, actionable advice that you can implement in your daily life. We believe that everyone has the right to feel safe and secure, and by arming yourself with knowledge and skills, you can significantly reduce your vulnerability and increase your confidence.

One of the key principles underlying this book is the importance of prevention. While self-defense techniques are undoubtedly valuable, avoiding dangerous situations altogether is often the most effective strategy. Therefore, we dedicate a significant portion of this handbook to risk assessment, situational awareness, and proactive measures you can take to minimize potential threats.

Furthermore, "Safe and Sound" takes a holistic approach to personal safety. We recognize that safety encompasses not only physical protection but also mental and emotional well-being. Throughout the book, you will find chapters devoted to stress management, assertiveness training, and conflict resolution – all of which are essential components of a comprehensive safety plan.

Another aspect that sets "Safe and Sound" apart is its accessibility. We have structured the content in a user-friendly format, with clear explanations, practical tips, and illustrative examples. Whether you prefer to read cover to cover or jump to specific topics of interest, you will find this handbook easy to navigate and apply to your life.

It's important to note that personal safety and self-defense are lifelong journeys. As such, this book serves as a foundation upon which you can continue to build and refine your skills over time. We encourage you to approach this material with an open mind and a willingness to learn, recognizing that each individual's safety needs may differ.

Lastly, we would like to express our gratitude to the experts, practitioners, and individuals who have contributed their insights and experiences to this handbook. Their expertise has been invaluable in shaping the content and ensuring its relevance and effectiveness.

In closing, we hope that "Safe and Sound" becomes a trusted resource that empowers you to take control of your safety and lead a life free from fear. Remember, safety is not a privilege reserved for a select few – it is a fundamental right that we all deserve. Let's embark on this journey together, towards a future where everyone can feel safe and sound.

Stay vigilant, stay empowered, and stay safe.

Sincerely,

[HARIKUMAR V T]

COPYWRITE WARNING

CONTENTS

CHAPTER 1.
UNDERSTANDING
PERSONAL SAFETY

The sun was just beginning to set, casting a warm golden glow over the quiet neighborhood. Sarah walked briskly along the familiar streets, her mind preoccupied with thoughts of her upcoming trip. She was excited about the adventure ahead but also cautious, remembering the safety tips her mother had always emphasized. As she turned the corner onto her street, she noticed a man walking towards her. He seemed harmless enough, but Sarah's instincts kicked in, and she subtly adjusted her path to give him a wider berth.

Personal safety is not just about being cautious in potentially dangerous situations; it's a mindset, a way of thinking and acting that can significantly reduce your risk of harm. In today's world, where threats can come from various sources, understanding personal safety is more critical than ever.

The Importance of Personal Safety

Personal safety encompasses a range of practices and strategies designed to protect individuals from harm. It includes physical safety, emotional well-being, and awareness of potential risks in different environments. Whether you're walking home alone at night, traveling to unfamiliar places, or interacting with strangers, being mindful of your personal safety can make a significant difference in your overall security and peace of mind.

For Sarah, growing up in a bustling city meant learning early on about the importance of personal safety. Her parents taught her simple yet effective strategies, such as always staying alert in public spaces, avoiding isolated areas, and trusting her instincts when something felt off. These lessons became ingrained in her daily life, shaping her behavior and decision-making process.

The Three Pillars of Personal Safety

To truly understand personal safety, it's essential to explore its three fundamental pillars: awareness, prevention, and response.

Awareness: The foundation of personal safety lies in being aware of your surroundings and potential threats. This includes paying attention to people, places, and situations that may pose risks. Sarah's habit of scanning her environment as she walked reflected this aspect of awareness. By staying alert and tuned into her surroundings, she could identify any potential dangers early on and take appropriate action.

Prevention: Prevention involves taking proactive steps to minimize risks and vulnerabilities. This can include simple measures such as locking doors and windows, avoiding risky behaviors like excessive drinking or drug use, and practicing good cyber hygiene to protect personal information online. Sarah's decision to adjust her path when she encountered the man on her street demonstrated a proactive approach to preventing potential threats.

Response: Despite our best efforts, there may be times when we encounter dangerous situations. Knowing how to respond effectively is crucial in such moments. This can include de-escalation techniques, self-defense skills, and knowing when to seek help from authorities or trusted individuals. Sarah had undergone self-defense training, which gave her confidence in her ability to protect herself if a situation escalated.

Building Your Personal Safety Toolkit

Just as a carpenter relies on a set of tools to build a sturdy structure, individuals can develop a personal safety toolkit to navigate life's challenges safely. This toolkit may include:

Education: Continuously educate yourself about personal safety best practices, self-defense techniques, and local laws and regulations. Attend workshops, read books, and stay informed about current safety trends.

Communication: Foster open and honest communication with family, friends, and colleagues about personal safety concerns. Discuss emergency plans, share safety tips, and support each other in staying vigilant.

Technology: Utilize technology to enhance your safety, such as mobile apps for tracking your location, emergency alert systems, and home security devices like cameras and alarms.

Physical Fitness: Maintain physical fitness and wellness, as they play a vital role in your ability to respond effectively in challenging situations. Regular exercise not only improves strength and endurance but also boosts confidence and mental resilience.

Mindfulness: Practice mindfulness and situational awareness in your daily life. Be present in the moment, trust your instincts, and avoid distractions that may compromise your safety.

As Sarah reached her doorstep, she felt a sense of relief knowing she had safely navigated her neighborhood once again. Reflecting on her journey, she realized that personal safety was not just a set of rules to follow but a way of life—a mindset that empowered her to take control of her well-being.

Understanding personal safety is about being proactive, informed, and prepared. It's about trusting your instincts, making smart choices, and knowing how to respond effectively in different situations. In the pages that follow, we will delve deeper into each aspect of personal safety, equipping you with the knowledge and tools to lead a safe and sound life.

Remember, safety begins with you. Stay aware, stay prepared, and stay safe.

CHAPTER 2. ASSESSING YOUR RISK PROFILE

I n the realm of personal safety and self-defense, one of the foundational steps is assessing your risk profile. Understanding the risks you face in different situations and environments is crucial for developing effective safety strategies. This article will provide a comprehensive guide to help you assess your risk profile and make informed decisions to enhance your safety and security.

Understanding Risk

Risk, in the context of personal safety, refers to the likelihood of encountering harmful or dangerous situations. These risks can vary widely based on factors such as your location, daily activities, personal habits, and the overall security of your environment. By evaluating these elements, you can gain insights into the specific risks you may encounter and take proactive measures to mitigate them.

Identifying Potential Risks

The first step in assessing your risk profile is identifying potential risks relevant to your life and surroundings. Consider the following areas:

Physical Environment: Evaluate the safety of your home, workplace, and frequented locations. Look for potential hazards such as poorly lit areas, lack of security measures, or proximity to high-crime areas.

Daily Activities: Reflect on your daily routines and activities. Are there times when you are more vulnerable, such as walking alone at night, using public transportation, or visiting unfamiliar places?

Social Interactions: Assess your social interactions and relationships. Are there individuals or situations that make you feel uncomfortable or unsafe? Pay attention to your instincts and intuition in these situations.

Digital Presence: Consider your online presence and digital habits. Are you mindful of privacy settings on social media? Do you practice safe browsing habits and protect sensitive information?

Conducting a Risk Assessment

Once you've identified potential risks, conduct a thorough risk assessment using the following steps:

Risk Identification: List all identified risks based on the categories mentioned earlier. Be specific and consider both immediate risks and long-term vulnerabilities.

Risk Analysis: Evaluate each identified risk in terms of its likelihood and potential impact. Use a scale (e.g., low, medium, high) to categorize risks based on their severity.

Risk Mitigation: Develop strategies to mitigate or reduce each identified risk. This may include practical measures such as improving home security, avoiding risky behaviors, or seeking support from trusted individuals or professionals.

Personal Safety Strategies

Based on your risk assessment, tailor your personal safety strategies to address specific areas of concern. Here are some key strategies to consider:

Home Safety: Install security systems, reinforce doors and windows, and maintain good lighting around your property. Develop emergency plans for various scenarios, such as fires, intrusions, or medical emergencies.

Travel Safety: Research destinations before traveling, avoid high-risk areas, and stay aware of local laws and customs. Keep important documents secure, use reputable transportation services, and share your itinerary with trusted contacts.

Social Awareness: Trust your instincts in social interactions and avoid situations or individuals that make you feel uneasy. Set boundaries, communicate assertively, and seek support if you feel threatened or harassed.

Digital Security: Use strong passwords, enable two-factor authentication, and update security software regularly. Be cautious of sharing personal information online and avoid clicking on suspicious links or emails.

Self-Defense Training: Consider enrolling in self-defense classes to learn practical skills for protecting yourself in threatening situations. Practice situational awareness and de-escalation techniques to defuse potential conflicts.

Ongoing Evaluation and Adjustment

Personal safety is not a one-time assessment but an ongoing process. Regularly review and update your risk profile as circumstances change or new risks emerge. Stay informed about safety trends, seek guidance from experts or professionals, and empower yourself with knowledge and skills to enhance your safety and self-defense capabilities.

Assessing your risk profile is a foundational step in creating a safe and secure environment for yourself. By identifying potential risks, conducting a thorough risk assessment, and implementing tailored safety strategies, you can mitigate threats and navigate life's challenges with confidence.

In the journey towards personal safety and self-defense, remember that awareness, preparation, and proactive measures are key elements. Stay vigilant, trust your instincts, and empower yourself to lead a safe and sound life.

CHAPTER 3. DEVELOPING A SAFETY MINDSET

In the quest for personal safety and self-defense, developing a safety mindset is paramount. A safety mindset goes beyond simple precautionary measures; it embodies a proactive approach to assessing risks, making informed decisions, and taking deliberate actions to protect oneself. This article will delve deep into the concept of developing a safety mindset, providing a comprehensive guide to empower individuals with the knowledge and strategies needed to navigate potential threats effectively.

Understanding the Safety Mindset

A safety mindset is a mental framework that prioritizes awareness, preparedness, and proactive measures to enhance personal safety and security. It involves adopting a cautious yet confident approach to daily life, recognizing potential risks, and taking steps to mitigate them. A safety mindset is not about living in fear but rather being mindful and empowered to respond effectively to challenging situations.

Key Elements of a Safety Mindset

Awareness: A safety mindset begins with heightened awareness of one's surroundings, potential threats, and vulnerabilities. It involves paying attention to details, trusting instincts, and staying attuned to changes in the environment.

Preparedness: Being prepared is a fundamental aspect of a safety mindset. This includes having emergency plans in place, knowing how to respond to different scenarios, and having access to resources and tools for self-defense and protection.

Proactivity: A safety mindset emphasizes proactive measures to minimize risks and prevent potential harm. This may involve making conscious decisions about where to go, who to trust, and how to navigate unfamiliar situations safely.

Empowerment: Central to a safety mindset is a sense of empowerment and self-reliance. It involves building confidence in one's abilities, seeking knowledge and training, and developing the skills needed to protect oneself and others.

Developing a Safety Mindset: Steps and Strategies

Assessing Risks: Begin by identifying potential risks in your daily life and surroundings. Consider factors such as your living environment, daily activities, social interactions, and digital presence. Conduct a thorough risk assessment to understand the specific threats you may face.

Education and Training: Educate yourself about personal safety best practices, self-defense techniques, and local laws and regulations. Enroll in self-defense classes, attend workshops, and seek guidance from experts in safety and security.

Building Awareness: Cultivate a habit of situational awareness by paying attention to your surroundings at all times. Notice details such as people's behavior, unusual activities, and potential danger signs. Trust your instincts and intuition.

Creating Safety Plans: Develop emergency plans for various scenarios, including home intrusions, natural disasters, medical emergencies, and social confrontations. Communicate these plans with trusted individuals and practice drills to ensure readiness.

Utilizing Technology: Leverage technology to enhance your safety, such as mobile apps for tracking your location, emergency alert systems, and personal safety devices like pepper sprays or alarms. Use secure communication channels and protect your digital information.

Practicing Self-Care: Prioritize your physical and mental well-being as part of your safety mindset. Maintain a healthy lifestyle, manage stress effectively, and seek support or counseling if needed. A strong mind and body contribute to better decision-making and resilience in challenging situations.

Engaging in Risk Management: Implement risk management strategies to reduce vulnerabilities and potential harm. This may include avoiding risky behaviors, setting boundaries in social interactions, and seeking help or reporting threats to authorities when necessary.

Continual Learning and Improvement: Stay informed about safety trends, new technologies, and best practices in personal safety and self-defense. Continuously update and refine your safety strategies based on feedback, experiences, and lessons learned.

Case Studies and Examples

Home Safety: Sarah, a single mother living in a suburban neighborhood, developed a safety mindset by installing security cameras, reinforcing doors and windows, and teaching her children about emergency protocols. When faced with a potential break-in, Sarah's preparedness and quick action prevented the intrusion and ensured her family's safety.

Travel Safety: Alex, a frequent traveler for work, adopted a safety mindset by researching destinations, avoiding high-risk areas, and carrying essential safety tools such as a travel alarm and emergency contacts. His vigilance and proactive measures helped him navigate unfamiliar environments safely and avoid potential threats.

Digital Security: Maya, a college student, practiced a safety mindset online by using strong passwords, avoiding public Wi-Fi networks, and being cautious about sharing personal information on social media. Her awareness and proactive approach protected her from cyber threats and identity theft.

Developing a safety mindset is a journey that requires dedication, awareness, and ongoing effort. By prioritizing awareness, preparedness, proactivity, and empowerment, individuals can enhance their personal safety and self-defense capabilities. Remember that a safety mindset is not about living in fear but rather being proactive and confident in your ability to navigate life's challenges safely.

Incorporate the strategies outlined in this guide into your daily life, seek additional training and resources as needed, and stay vigilant in assessing and managing risks. With a strong safety mindset, you can lead a safer, more secure, and empowered life.

CHAPTER 4. ENHANCING SITUATIONAL AWARENESS

Situational awareness is a critical skill that forms the cornerstone of personal safety and self-defense. It involves being mindful of your surroundings, recognizing potential threats, and making informed decisions to protect yourself and others. This article will provide a comprehensive guide to enhancing situational awareness, equipping readers with the knowledge and strategies needed to navigate various environments safely.

Understanding Situational Awareness

Situational awareness refers to the ability to perceive, comprehend, and anticipate events and developments in one's environment. It involves actively observing and processing information about people, objects, and circumstances to assess potential risks and make effective decisions. Situational awareness is a dynamic process that requires constant vigilance and attention to detail.

Key Components of Situational Awareness

Perception: The first step in situational awareness is perceiving relevant information in your environment. This includes using your senses (sight, hearing, touch, etc.) to gather data about people, objects, and events around you.

Comprehension: Once you have gathered information, the next step is to comprehend its meaning and significance. This involves analyzing patterns, assessing potential threats, and understanding the context of the situation.

Projection: Projection refers to anticipating future developments based on your understanding of the current situation. It involves predicting potential outcomes and planning proactive responses to mitigate risks.

Enhancing Situational Awareness: Strategies and Techniques

Stay Alert and Observant: Cultivate a habit of being alert and observant in your daily life. Pay attention to details such as people's behavior, body language, and unusual activities. Notice changes in your environment and trust your instincts if something feels off.

Scan Your Environment: Practice scanning your surroundings regularly, especially in unfamiliar or potentially risky environments. Use a 360-degree approach to observe people, exits, emergency resources, and potential hiding spots.

Maintain a Low Profile: Avoid drawing unnecessary attention to yourself and minimize distractions that may compromise your awareness. Stay focused on the task at hand and avoid excessive use of electronic devices in public spaces.

Trust Your Intuition: Learn to trust your instincts and gut feelings. If something doesn't seem right or feels unsafe, listen to your intuition and take appropriate action, such as changing your route, seeking help, or leaving the area.

Use Peripheral Vision: Expand your awareness by using peripheral vision to detect movement and activity in your surroundings. Practice widening your visual field and incorporating peripheral cues into your situational assessment.

Stay Informed: Stay informed about current events, safety trends, and potential threats in your area. Follow reputable news sources, participate in community safety initiatives, and attend safety workshops or seminars.

Practice Mindfulness: Cultivate mindfulness and present-moment awareness in your daily activities. Be fully engaged in your surroundings, avoid multitasking when safety is a concern, and minimize distractions that may hinder your situational awareness.

Plan Escape Routes: Always have an exit strategy and escape routes in mind, especially in crowded or confined spaces. Identify multiple exit points, know alternative routes, and be prepared to evacuate quickly if necessary.

Real-Life Applications of Enhanced Situational Awareness

Public Transportation: When using public transportation, such as buses or trains, enhance your situational awareness by choosing well-lit areas, staying near exits, and keeping valuables secure. Be aware of your fellow passengers and report any suspicious behavior to authorities.

Nighttime Safety: When walking alone at night, boost your situational awareness by staying in well-populated, well-lit areas. Avoid distractions like headphones or excessive phone use, and trust your instincts if you feel unsafe or threatened.

Social Gatherings: At social gatherings or events, practice situational awareness by scanning the crowd, noting emergency exits, and staying mindful of your surroundings. Be cautious of strangers and maintain control over your drinks and personal belongings.

Workplace Safety: In the workplace, enhance situational awareness by familiarizing yourself with emergency protocols, identifying safety hazards, and reporting any suspicious or concerning behavior to HR or security personnel.

Enhancing situational awareness is a vital skill that empowers individuals to assess risks, make informed decisions, and respond effectively in challenging situations. By incorporating the strategies and techniques outlined in this guide into your daily life, you can significantly improve your personal safety and self-defense capabilities.

Remember that situational awareness is not about living in fear but rather being prepared and proactive in safeguarding yourself and others. Stay alert, stay informed, and stay safe.

CHAPTER 5. RECOGNIZING COMMON THREATS

I n today's world, being able to recognize common threats is essential for personal safety and self-defense. Whether you're at home, in public spaces, or traveling, understanding potential dangers and knowing how to respond effectively can significantly reduce your risk of harm. This article will provide a comprehensive guide to recognizing common threats, empowering readers with the knowledge and awareness needed to stay safe and sound.

Types of Common Threats

Physical Threats: Physical threats involve direct harm to your person, such as assault, robbery, or physical altercations. These threats can occur in various environments, including streets, parks, public transportation, or even in your own home.

Verbal Threats: Verbal threats encompass threats of harm or violence communicated through words, gestures, or actions. This may include intimidation, harassment, bullying, or verbal abuse, which can occur in social settings, workplaces, or online interactions.

Environmental Threats: Environmental threats are hazards or dangers present in your surroundings, such as natural disasters, hazardous materials, unsafe structures, or environmental pollution. These threats require awareness and preparedness to mitigate risks.

Digital Threats: Digital threats involve risks related to technology and online activities, such as cyberbullying, identity theft, phishing scams, malware attacks, and online predators. Protecting yourself from digital threats requires cybersecurity awareness and safe online practices.

Recognizing Common Threats: Key Indicators and Signs

Suspicious Behavior: Be vigilant of individuals exhibiting suspicious behavior, such as loitering near entrances or exits, watching others closely, or acting furtively. Trust your instincts and pay attention to body language cues that may indicate potential threats.

Aggressive or Hostile Actions: Recognize signs of aggression or hostility, such as raised voices, threatening gestures, invasion of personal space, or confrontational posturing. Take these cues seriously and consider de-escalation strategies or seeking assistance if necessary.

Unusual Objects or Packages: Be cautious of unusual objects or packages in public spaces or near your surroundings. Report any suspicious items to authorities and avoid handling or approaching them yourself.

Changes in Environment: Stay aware of changes in your environment, such as sudden disruptions, alarms, or unusual noises. These may indicate emergencies, security breaches, or potential threats requiring immediate action or evacuation.

Cybersecurity Risks: Recognize common cybersecurity risks, such as phishing emails, suspicious links or attachments, unauthorized access attempts, and unusual online behavior. Practice safe browsing habits, use strong passwords, and employ cybersecurity tools to protect your digital information.

Responding to Common Threats: Safety Strategies and Actions

Stay Calm and Assess the Situation: In the face of a threat, stay calm and assess the situation objectively. Avoid escalating conflicts or responding impulsively, and prioritize your safety and well-being.

Seek Assistance: If you perceive a threat or danger, seek assistance from authorities, security personnel, or trusted individuals. Report suspicious activities or behaviors promptly and provide detailed information to aid in addressing the threat.

De-escalation Techniques: When confronted with verbal or potentially physical threats, employ de-escalation techniques to defuse tensions and resolve conflicts peacefully. Use active listening, remain respectful, and avoid provoking further aggression.

Escape and Evacuation: If faced with an immediate threat or danger, prioritize escape and evacuation to a safer location. Identify exit routes, emergency exits, and safe havens in your environment, and evacuate calmly and swiftly if necessary.

Self-Defense Measures: Consider learning self-defense techniques and strategies to protect yourself in physical confrontations. Practice situational awareness, assertive communication, and physical techniques for self-protection if escape is not possible.

Real-Life Examples and Case Studies

Recognizing Suspicious Behavior: Sarah, a college student, recognized suspicious behavior when a stranger followed her closely on a deserted street. She quickly crossed the street, entered a well-lit area with people, and called a friend for assistance, avoiding a potentially dangerous situation.

Responding to Verbal Threats: Alex, a retail worker, used de-escalation techniques when faced with a customer's aggressive behavior. He remained calm, listened attentively to the customer's concerns, and addressed them respectfully, diffusing the situation and maintaining a safe environment.

Handling Cybersecurity Risks: Maya, an office manager, identified a phishing email targeting her company's employees. She promptly alerted the IT department, educated staff about phishing scams, and implemented cybersecurity measures to prevent unauthorized access, safeguarding sensitive data.

Recognizing common threats is a fundamental skill that empowers individuals to protect themselves and others in various situations. By being aware of key indicators and signs of threats, understanding safety strategies and actions, and staying vigilant in daily life, you can enhance your personal safety and self-defense capabilities.

Incorporate the information and guidance provided in this article into your daily routines, seek additional training or resources as needed, and empower yourself with the knowledge and awareness to recognize and respond effectively to common threats. Remember that prevention, awareness, and preparedness are key elements in staying safe and sound in today's dynamic world.

CHAPTER 6. AVOIDING DANGEROUS SITUATIONS

Avoiding dangerous situations is a critical aspect of personal safety and self-defense. By recognizing potential risks and taking proactive measures to steer clear of harm, individuals can significantly reduce their vulnerability to threats. This article serves as a comprehensive guide, offering strategies and techniques to help readers avoid dangerous situations and enhance their overall safety and well-being.

Understanding Dangerous Situations

Dangerous situations encompass a wide range of scenarios that pose risks to personal safety and security. These may include physical confrontations, verbal altercations, hazardous environments, cyber threats, and more. Recognizing the signs and indicators of potential danger is crucial in preventing harm and maintaining a safe environment.

Common Types of Dangerous Situations

Physical Confrontations: These involve direct physical threats or attacks, such as assaults, robberies, or confrontations with aggressive individuals.

Verbal Altercations: Verbal conflicts or arguments that escalate into threatening or hostile exchanges, leading to potential confrontations.

Environmental Hazards: Unsafe or hazardous environments, such as poorly lit areas, unstable structures, natural disaster-prone areas, or areas with high crime rates.

Cyber Threats: Online risks and threats, including cyberbullying, identity theft, phishing scams, malware attacks, and online predators.

Strategies for Avoiding Dangerous Situations

Situational Awareness: Maintain a high level of situational awareness by staying alert, observing your surroundings, and being mindful of potential threats. Notice changes in the environment, unusual behaviors, or suspicious activities.

Trust Your Instincts: Trust your gut feelings and intuition. If something feels off or unsafe, listen to your instincts and take action to remove yourself from the situation.

Plan Ahead: Before engaging in activities or visiting unfamiliar places, research and plan ahead. Identify potential risks and hazards, map out escape routes, and have a contingency plan in case of emergencies.

Avoid Risky Areas and Behaviors: Stay away from high-crime areas, poorly lit streets, secluded or isolated locations, and places known for violence or criminal activities. Avoid engaging in risky behaviors that may attract unwanted attention or increase your vulnerability.

Use Safe Transportation: Choose safe and reputable transportation options, especially when traveling alone or at night. Use well-lit and populated routes, and avoid walking or waiting in isolated areas.

Limit Digital Exposure: Protect yourself from cyber threats by practicing safe online habits. Use strong passwords, be cautious of sharing personal information, avoid clicking on suspicious links or emails, and use reputable cybersecurity tools.

Stay Sober and Alert: Avoid excessive alcohol or drug consumption, as it can impair judgment and reaction times, making you more vulnerable to dangerous situations.

Establish Boundaries: Set clear boundaries in your interactions with others and assertively communicate your limits. Avoid getting drawn into conflicts or arguments that may escalate into dangerous situations.

Real-Life Examples and Case Studies

Avoiding Physical Confrontations: John, a college student, avoided a potential physical altercation by walking away from a heated argument and seeking help from campus security. His quick thinking and avoidance of further conflict prevented violence.

Navigating Hazardous Environments: Maria, a hiker, stayed safe in a hazardous environment by researching the trail beforehand, carrying essential safety gear, and staying aware of weather conditions. Her preparation and caution helped her avoid dangerous situations.

Cybersecurity Vigilance: David, an office worker, avoided falling victim to a phishing scam by recognizing suspicious emails, verifying sources, and reporting the threat to IT security. His vigilance protected sensitive data and prevented potential cyber attacks.

Avoiding dangerous situations is a proactive approach to personal safety and self-defense. By understanding common types of threats, practicing situational awareness, planning ahead, and using caution in various environments, individuals can reduce their risk of harm and stay safe in their daily lives.

Incorporate the strategies and techniques outlined in this article into your personal safety practices, seek additional training or resources as needed, and empower yourself with the knowledge and skills to avoid dangerous situations effectively. Remember that prevention and awareness are key elements in staying safe and sound.

CHAPTER 7.
ASSERTIVENESS
TRAINING

Assertiveness training plays a vital role in empowering individuals to protect themselves, assert boundaries, and navigate challenging situations with confidence. In the context of personal safety and self-defense, assertiveness is a valuable skill that allows individuals to communicate effectively, set boundaries, and respond assertively to potential threats. This article serves as a comprehensive guide to assertiveness training, offering strategies, techniques, and practical advice to help readers enhance their assertiveness and strengthen their personal safety and self-defense capabilities.

Understanding Assertiveness

Assertiveness is the ability to express thoughts, feelings, and needs in a clear, confident, and respectful manner. It involves standing up for oneself, setting boundaries, and communicating assertively without being aggressive or passive. In the context of personal safety and self-defense, assertiveness enables individuals to assert their rights, say "no" when necessary, and take proactive measures to protect themselves from harm.

Key Elements of Assertiveness Training

Self-Confidence: Building self-confidence is a foundational element of assertiveness training. Believing in oneself, recognizing strengths, and valuing one's opinions and feelings are essential for assertive communication and behavior.

Effective Communication: Assertiveness training emphasizes effective communication skills, such as active listening, clear articulation of thoughts and feelings, using "I" statements, and maintaining eye contact and body language that conveys confidence.

Setting Boundaries: Assertiveness involves setting and maintaining personal boundaries, which define acceptable behaviors, actions, and treatment from others. Learning to say "no" assertively and without guilt is a key aspect of boundary-setting.

Conflict Resolution: Assertiveness training equips individuals with conflict resolution skills, including assertive negotiation, de-escalation techniques, and finding mutually acceptable solutions to conflicts or disagreements.

Self-Advocacy: Assertive individuals advocate for their needs, rights, and well-being. They assertively express concerns, seek support or assistance when needed, and take proactive steps to address challenges or threats.

Strategies for Assertiveness Training

Self-Reflection: Start by reflecting on your strengths, values, and areas where you'd like to improve assertiveness. Identify specific situations or behaviors where assertiveness is needed, such as setting boundaries, expressing needs, or handling conflicts.

Assertive Communication Techniques: Practice assertive communication techniques, such as using "I" statements to express feelings and needs ("I feel...," "I need..."), active listening to understand others' perspectives, and maintaining a calm and composed demeanor.

Role-Playing: Engage in role-playing exercises to practice assertive communication in various scenarios. Role-play situations where you need to assert boundaries, say "no" assertively, or handle confrontations calmly and confidently.

Boundary-Setting: Define and communicate your personal boundaries clearly and assertively. Practice saying "no" without feeling guilty, and be firm in upholding boundaries that protect your physical, emotional, and mental well-being.

Conflict Resolution Skills: Develop conflict resolution skills by learning to express concerns assertively, listen actively to others' viewpoints, seek compromise or solutions that meet everyone's needs, and avoid escalating conflicts through aggression or passivity.

Positive Self-Talk: Cultivate positive self-talk and affirmations to boost self-confidence and reinforce assertive behavior. Replace self-doubt or negative beliefs with empowering statements that affirm your worth and capabilities.

Seek Support: Consider seeking support from assertiveness training workshops, counseling, or self-help resources that focus on building assertiveness skills. Surround yourself with supportive individuals who encourage and reinforce assertive behavior.

Benefits of Assertiveness Training for Personal Safety and Self-Defense

Increased Confidence: Assertiveness training boosts self-confidence, empowering individuals to trust their instincts, make decisions confidently, and take proactive steps to ensure personal safety.

Improved Communication: Assertive communication enhances clarity, reduces misunderstandings, and fosters respectful interactions, which are essential for effective self-defense strategies and conflict resolution.

Enhanced Boundary-Setting: Assertiveness training strengthens boundary-setting skills, enabling individuals to assert their limits, protect their personal space, and prevent potential threats or intrusions.

Effective De-escalation: Assertive individuals are skilled at de-escalating conflicts and defusing potentially volatile situations through calm, assertive communication and problem-solving approaches.

Empowerment: Assertiveness training empowers individuals to advocate for themselves, assert their rights, and take control of their personal safety and well-being.

Real-Life Examples and Case Studies

Boundary-Setting: Sarah, a college student, attended assertiveness training workshops and learned to set boundaries with peers who pressured her into risky behaviors. By assertively saying "no" and standing firm in her decisions, she protected herself from harm and maintained her integrity.

Conflict Resolution: Alex, a manager, applied assertiveness training principles to resolve conflicts among team members. By fostering open communication, active listening, and assertive problem-solving, he created a harmonious and productive work environment.

De-escalation Skills: Maya, a customer service representative, utilized assertiveness training techniques to de-escalate irate customers. Through empathetic listening, assertive responses, and finding mutually agreeable solutions, she diffused tensions and maintained positive customer relationships.

Assertiveness training is a valuable tool for personal safety and self-defense, equipping individuals with the skills and confidence to navigate challenging situations assertively and effectively. By practicing assertive communication, setting boundaries, resolving conflicts peacefully, and advocating for themselves, individuals can enhance their personal safety, strengthen their self-defense capabilities, and lead empowered lives.

Incorporate the strategies and techniques outlined in this article into your assertiveness training journey, seek additional support or resources as needed, and empower yourself to assert your rights, protect your boundaries, and ensure your safety and well-being.

CHAPTER 8. CONFLICT RESOLUTION TECHNIQUES

Conflict resolution techniques are indispensable tools for navigating challenging situations, diffusing conflicts, and promoting harmony in interpersonal interactions. In the context of personal safety and self-defense, mastering effective conflict resolution skills can empower individuals to de-escalate conflicts, assert boundaries, and protect themselves from harm. This article serves as a comprehensive guide to conflict resolution techniques, offering strategies, principles, and practical advice to help readers enhance their conflict resolution abilities and strengthen their overall safety and well-being.

Understanding Conflict

Conflict is a natural part of human interactions and can arise in various situations, including disagreements, misunderstandings, power struggles, or clashes of interests. Conflict can manifest in verbal, non-verbal, or physical forms, and effective conflict resolution involves addressing underlying issues, finding common ground, and reaching mutually satisfactory solutions.

Key Elements of Conflict Resolution

Effective Communication: Clear and respectful communication is essential for resolving conflicts. Active listening, empathy, and assertive yet non-confrontational expression of thoughts and feelings are key components of effective communication in conflict resolution.

Empathy and Understanding: Empathy involves putting oneself in another's shoes, understanding their perspective, and acknowledging their emotions and concerns. Demonstrating empathy fosters understanding and builds rapport in conflict resolution.

Assertiveness: Assertiveness is the ability to express oneself confidently, assert boundaries, and advocate for one's needs and rights without being aggressive or passive. Assertive communication is crucial for addressing conflicts assertively and effectively.

Problem-Solving Skills: Conflict resolution often requires problem-solving skills to identify underlying issues, brainstorm solutions, evaluate options, and implement mutually agreeable strategies to resolve conflicts.

Emotional Regulation: Managing emotions effectively is essential in conflict resolution. Maintaining calmness, controlling emotional reactions, and staying focused on finding solutions contribute to successful conflict resolution outcomes.

Conflict Resolution Techniques and Strategies

Active Listening: Listen attentively to the other party's perspective without interrupting or judging. Paraphrase their statements to ensure understanding and show empathy by acknowledging their emotions and concerns.

Seek Common Ground: Identify shared interests or goals that both parties can agree upon. Focus on areas of agreement to build rapport and create a foundation for resolving differences.

Clarify Misunderstandings: Address any misunderstandings or miscommunications by seeking clarification, asking open-ended questions, and validating the other party's viewpoints before presenting your own.

Use "I" Statements: Express your thoughts, feelings, and needs using "I" statements to take ownership of your perspective without blaming or accusing the other party. For example, "I feel upset when..." or "I need..."

Assertive Communication: Be assertive in expressing your boundaries, concerns, and expectations while respecting the other party's rights and perspectives. Use assertive body language, maintain eye contact, and speak confidently and clearly.

Collaborative Problem-Solving: Collaborate with the other party to brainstorm solutions, explore alternatives, and negotiate mutually acceptable agreements. Focus on win-win outcomes that address the interests and needs of both parties.

Take Breaks When Necessary: If emotions escalate or tensions rise, take breaks to cool down and regain composure before continuing the conflict resolution process. Use breaks as opportunities for reflection and self-regulation.

Apologize and Forgive: Offer genuine apologies for any mistakes or misunderstandings on your part, and be open to forgiving others for their contributions to the conflict. Apologizing and forgiving promote reconciliation and closure in conflict resolution.

Benefits of Effective Conflict Resolution for Personal Safety

De-escalation of Tensions: Effective conflict resolution techniques help de-escalate tensions and prevent conflicts from escalating into harmful or violent situations.

Assertive Boundary-Setting: Conflict resolution skills empower individuals to assert their boundaries assertively, protect their personal space, and prevent potential threats or intrusions.

Enhanced Communication: Improved communication through conflict resolution fosters understanding, reduces misunderstandings, and promotes respectful interactions, which are crucial for personal safety and self-defense.

Negotiation and Compromise: Conflict resolution techniques enable individuals to negotiate and find compromises that meet everyone's needs, leading to mutually beneficial outcomes and harmonious relationships.

Real-Life Examples and Case Studies

Workplace Conflict Resolution: Alex, a manager, utilized conflict resolution techniques to address conflicts among team members. By facilitating open communication, clarifying misunderstandings, and finding compromises, he promoted a positive work environment and enhanced team cohesion.

Family Conflict Resolution: Sarah, a parent, applied conflict resolution skills to resolve conflicts with her teenage child. Through active listening, empathy, and collaborative problem-solving, she strengthened their relationship and fostered mutual respect.

Community Conflict Resolution: Maya, a community leader, employed conflict resolution techniques to address disputes among community members. By facilitating dialogue, seeking common ground, and promoting understanding, she promoted harmony and cooperation within the community.

Conflict resolution techniques are invaluable tools for personal safety and self-defense, empowering individuals to navigate conflicts assertively, communicate effectively, and foster harmonious relationships. By practicing active listening, empathy, assertive communication, and collaborative problem-solving, individuals can de-escalate conflicts, assert boundaries, and protect themselves from harm.

Incorporate the strategies and techniques outlined in this article into your conflict resolution toolkit, seek additional training or resources as needed, and empower yourself to resolve conflicts peacefully, promote personal safety, and enhance your overall well-being.

CHAPTER 9. EFFECTIVE COMMUNICATION SKILLS

In the realm of personal safety and self-defense, effective communication skills are an invaluable asset. Whether it's de-escalating a potentially dangerous situation or conveying your needs clearly to others, mastering the art of communication can significantly enhance your safety and well-being. This chapter delves into the principles and strategies of effective communication, providing insights and techniques that can be applied in various contexts.

Understanding Communication

Communication is the process of exchanging information, thoughts, and feelings between individuals. It encompasses verbal and non-verbal elements, including gestures, facial expressions, tone of voice, and body language. Effective communication goes beyond mere words; it involves active listening, empathy, clarity, and assertiveness.

Key Principles of Effective Communication

Active Listening: One of the cornerstones of effective communication is active listening. This involves giving your full attention to the speaker, maintaining eye contact, nodding or using other non-verbal cues to show understanding, and refraining from interrupting. By actively listening, you demonstrate respect and create a conducive environment for meaningful dialogue.

Empathy: Empathy is the ability to understand and share the feelings of another person. It plays a crucial role in communication by fostering connection and rapport. When communicating, strive to put yourself in the other person's shoes, acknowledge their emotions, and respond with sensitivity and understanding.

Clarity: Clear and concise communication is essential, especially in high-stress or potentially confrontational situations. Use simple language, avoid jargon or ambiguity, and ensure that your message is easily understood. Clarify any misunderstandings promptly and encourage feedback to confirm mutual understanding.

Assertiveness: Assertiveness involves expressing your thoughts, feelings, and needs confidently and respectfully. It is distinct from aggression or passivity, as it emphasizes standing up for yourself while considering the rights and perspectives of others. Practice assertive communication by using "I" statements, stating your boundaries clearly, and addressing conflicts constructively.

Communication Strategies for Personal Safety

De-Escalation Techniques: In situations where tensions are rising or conflicts are escalating, de-escalation techniques can defuse hostility and promote calmness. These techniques include maintaining a calm demeanor, using soothing or empathetic language, acknowledging the other person's concerns, and seeking common ground or solutions.

Boundary Setting: Clearly communicating and enforcing personal boundaries is crucial for maintaining safety and self-respect. Assertively communicate your boundaries regarding physical contact, personal space, and acceptable behavior. Be firm yet respectful in upholding these boundaries, and seek support or intervention if they are violated.

Conflict Resolution: Effective communication plays a pivotal role in resolving conflicts peacefully and constructively. When faced with a conflict, listen actively to all parties involved, acknowledge differing perspectives, and focus on finding mutually acceptable solutions. Avoid escalating conflicts through aggressive language or actions, and prioritize open dialogue and compromise.

Verbal Self-Defense: Verbal self-defense involves using communication skills to protect yourself from verbal aggression, manipulation, or intimidation. Techniques include maintaining a confident posture and tone, setting clear boundaries, using assertive language, deflecting personal attacks calmly, and disengaging from unproductive or harmful interactions.

Practical Tips for Enhancing Communication Skills

Practice active listening in everyday conversations, focusing on understanding rather than formulating responses.

Develop empathy by considering others' perspectives and experiences, especially in challenging or conflict-prone situations.

Hone your clarity by using simple language, avoiding vague or ambiguous statements, and checking for understanding.

Role-play various scenarios to enhance assertiveness and confidence in expressing your needs and boundaries.

Seek feedback from trusted individuals to identify areas for improvement and refine your communication skills.

Effective communication skills are indispensable tools for personal safety, conflict resolution, and fostering healthy relationships. By cultivating active listening, empathy, clarity, and assertiveness, individuals can navigate challenging situations with confidence and resilience. Integrating communication strategies into daily life empowers individuals to communicate effectively, set boundaries, and contribute to safer and more harmonious environments.

CHAPTER 10. MANAGING FEAR AND ANXIETY

Fear and anxiety are natural responses to perceived threats or dangers, playing a crucial role in our survival instincts. However, when left unchecked, they can hinder our ability to respond effectively to challenging situations. This chapter explores strategies and techniques for managing fear and anxiety, empowering individuals to maintain composure, make informed decisions, and enhance personal safety.

Understanding Fear and Anxiety

Fear is a primal emotion triggered by real or imagined threats, activating the body's fight-or-flight response. It can manifest as feelings of dread, panic, or unease, often accompanied by physical symptoms such as increased heart rate, sweating, and shallow breathing. Anxiety, on the other hand, is a persistent sense of apprehension or worry about future events or uncertainties.

The Impact of Fear and Anxiety on Personal Safety

While fear and anxiety can prompt vigilance and caution, they can also impair judgment and decision-making in high-stress situations. Unmanaged fear may lead to panic reactions, aggression, or freeze responses, compromising one's ability to assess risks accurately and respond effectively to threats. Learning to manage fear and anxiety is essential for maintaining clarity of thought, controlling emotions, and taking appropriate actions to ensure personal safety.

Strategies for Managing Fear and Anxiety

Mindfulness and Relaxation Techniques: Mindfulness practices, such as deep breathing, meditation, and progressive muscle relaxation, can help reduce stress and promote a sense of calmness. Incorporate regular mindfulness exercises into your daily routine to build resilience and manage anxiety effectively.

Cognitive Restructuring: Cognitive restructuring involves identifying and challenging negative or irrational thoughts that contribute to fear and anxiety. Replace catastrophic thinking with realistic assessments of risks and potential outcomes, focusing on problem-solving and coping strategies rather than dwelling on worst-case scenarios.

Exposure Therapy: Gradual exposure to feared situations or stimuli can help desensitize individuals to fear and anxiety. Start with manageable steps, gradually increasing exposure levels while practicing relaxation techniques to manage discomfort. Over time, exposure therapy can reduce fear responses and increase confidence in facing challenging situations.

Physical Exercise: Regular physical exercise is an effective way to reduce stress, anxiety, and tension. Engage in activities such as walking, jogging, yoga, or martial arts to release endorphins, improve mood, and enhance overall well-being. Physical fitness also contributes to increased resilience and self-confidence.

Seeking Support: Don't hesitate to seek support from trusted friends, family members, or mental health professionals when dealing with overwhelming fear or anxiety. Talking about your feelings, receiving validation, and exploring coping strategies can provide valuable support and guidance.

Practical Tips for Managing Fear and Anxiety

Practice deep breathing exercises during moments of stress or anxiety to promote relaxation and calmness.

Challenge negative thoughts by asking yourself if they are based on facts or assumptions, and reframe them in a more realistic light.

Gradually expose yourself to feared situations or triggers, starting with small steps and utilizing relaxation techniques as needed.

Engage in regular physical activity to reduce stress hormones, improve mood, and boost resilience.

Develop a support network of understanding individuals who can offer encouragement, empathy, and practical advice.

Managing fear and anxiety is essential for personal safety, well-being, and resilience in challenging circumstances. By practicing mindfulness, cognitive restructuring, exposure therapy, physical exercise, and seeking support, individuals can effectively cope with fear and anxiety, make informed decisions, and respond calmly and confidently to potential threats. Integrating these strategies into daily life empowers individuals to navigate uncertainties with resilience, courage, and a sense of empowerment, contributing to a safer and more secure environment overall.

CHAPTER 11. SELF-DEFENSE BASICS

Stance and Movement

Self-defense is a vital skillset that empowers individuals to protect themselves and others in challenging or threatening situations. Central to effective self-defense techniques are proper stance and movement, which form the foundation for executing defensive maneuvers, maintaining balance, and maximizing physical strength. This chapter delves into the essential principles of stance and movement in self-defense, providing practical insights and strategies for developing a solid defensive posture and mobility.

Understanding Stance in Self-Defense

A proper stance is crucial in self-defense as it establishes a stable and balanced position from which to react and respond to potential threats. The key elements of a good defensive stance include:

Feet Position: Stand with your feet shoulder-width apart to maintain balance and stability. Distribute your weight evenly between both feet, keeping them slightly bent to facilitate quick movements.

Knee Flexion: Maintain a slight bend in your knees to absorb impact and facilitate mobility. Avoid locking your knees, as this can reduce your ability to move quickly and efficiently.

Hip Alignment: Keep your hips squared with your shoulders, facing the direction of the potential threat. This alignment allows for fluid movement and maximizes your defensive reach.

Upper Body Position: Position your upper body in a relaxed yet alert posture. Keep your hands up near your face, elbows bent, and chin tucked to protect vital areas such as the head and neck.

Eye Contact: Maintain eye contact with the potential threat while remaining aware of your surroundings. Focus on assessing the situation and identifying potential escape routes or defensive strategies.

Benefits of a Proper Stance in Self-Defense

Balance and Stability: A good stance provides a solid foundation, allowing you to maintain balance and stability during defensive maneuvers or counterattacks.

Mobility: Proper positioning of the feet and knees enables quick and agile movement, essential for evading strikes or creating distance from an attacker.

Defensive Reach: An aligned hip and upper body position extend your defensive reach, making it easier to block or deflect incoming attacks.

Protection: Keeping your hands up near your face and chin tucked offers protection to vulnerable areas, reducing the risk of injury during a confrontation.

Fundamentals of Movement in Self-Defense

In addition to a proper stance, effective movement is essential for self-defense, enabling you to evade threats, create distance, and reposition yourself strategically. Key principles of movement in self-defense include:

Footwork: Mastering footwork is crucial for maintaining mobility and agility in self-defense scenarios. Practice moving forward, backward, sideways, and diagonally while maintaining balance and a defensive stance.

Use small, quick steps to adjust your position and respond to changing dynamics.

Angles and Circles: Utilize angles and circular movements to avoid direct confrontation and create openings for counterattacks. Pivot on your feet to change directions swiftly, maintaining awareness of your surroundings and potential escape routes.

Evasion Techniques: Learn evasion techniques such as bobbing and weaving, slipping, and ducking to avoid incoming strikes or grabs. These techniques help minimize the impact of attacks and create opportunities to counter effectively.

Retreat and Re-engage: Know when to retreat to a safer position and reassess the situation before deciding to re-engage or seek assistance. Retreat strategically to create distance from the threat while remaining vigilant and ready to defend if necessary.

Use of Obstacles: Utilize obstacles in your environment, such as furniture or barriers, to create barriers between yourself and the threat. Use them strategically to impede the attacker's movements and buy time to assess and respond effectively.

Practical Application and Training Tips

Visualization and Simulation: Visualize potential self-defense scenarios and practice your stance and movement techniques in simulated environments. Enlist the help of a training partner or instructor to create realistic scenarios and receive feedback on your defensive skills.

Drills and Exercises: Incorporate drills and exercises that focus on stance and movement into your self-defense training regimen. Practice footwork drills, evasion techniques, and scenario-based simulations to develop muscle memory and improve reflexes.

Speed and Precision: Focus on executing movements with speed, precision, and control. Emphasize the importance of maintaining a defensive posture while moving fluidly and decisively in response to threats.

Feedback and Correction: Solicit feedback from instructors or training partners to identify areas for improvement in your stance and movement. Be open to constructive criticism and make adjustments to refine your defensive techniques over time.

Mastering the basics of stance and movement is essential for effective self-defense, enabling individuals to respond confidently and decisively in threatening situations. By developing a solid defensive posture, mastering footwork and mobility techniques, and practicing evasion strategies, individuals can enhance their ability to protect themselves and others. Integrating these fundamentals into regular self-defense training empowers individuals to navigate potentially dangerous scenarios with confidence, agility, and strategic awareness, contributing to a safer and more prepared community overall.

CHAPTER 12. DEFENSIVE TECHNIQUES FOR PHYSICAL ATTACKS

I n the realm of personal safety and self-defense, understanding and mastering defensive techniques for physical attacks are crucial skills. These techniques empower individuals to protect themselves effectively in various confrontational situations, ranging from unarmed assaults to physical altercations. This chapter explores a range of defensive techniques, including blocks, strikes, joint locks, and escapes, providing practical insights and strategies for enhancing personal safety and self-defense proficiency.

Understanding Defensive Techniques

Defensive techniques are maneuvers or actions employed to protect oneself from physical harm during an attack. These techniques are designed to neutralize threats, create opportunities for escape, and minimize the risk of injury. Effective defensive techniques require a combination of awareness, timing, skill, and confidence in responding to different types of attacks.

Types of Defensive Techniques

Blocks: Blocks are defensive maneuvers used to intercept and deflect incoming strikes or attacks. Common blocking techniques include:

High Block: Used to defend against overhead or high-angle strikes, such as punches or weapon attacks aimed at the head or shoulders.

Low Block: Employed to protect against low-level attacks, such as kicks or strikes aimed at the legs or midsection.

Outside Block: Used to deflect attacks coming from the outside, such as wide swings or hooks.

Strikes: Defensive strikes are offensive movements executed in response to an attack, aiming to disable or incapacitate the attacker. Common striking techniques include:

Palm Strike: A powerful strike delivered with the palm of the hand, targeting vulnerable areas such as the nose, throat, or solar plexus.

Elbow Strike: A close-range strike using the elbow, effective for close-quarters combat and delivering significant impact.

Knee Strike: A powerful strike using the knee, targeting the groin, abdomen, or thighs of the attacker.

Joint Locks: Joint locks are grappling techniques that immobilize or control an attacker by manipulating their joints. Common joint locks include:

Wrist Lock: Applied to the wrist joint, allowing control and restraint of the attacker's arm movements.

Arm Bar: A lock applied to the elbow joint, exerting pressure to immobilize the attacker's arm and create a submission hold.

Shoulder Lock: Targets the shoulder joint, restricting the attacker's arm movements and providing leverage for control or takedowns.

Escapes: Escape techniques are maneuvers used to break free from grabs, holds, or immobilizing positions. Common escape techniques include:

Wrist Release: Techniques to break free from wrist grabs or holds, using leverage, twists, or strikes to release the grip.

Bear Hug Escape: Strategies to escape from a bear hug or clinch position, including strikes, leverage, and shifting body weight.

Ground Escape: Techniques to escape from ground positions, such as mounts or pins, using bridging, shrimping, or sweeps.

Practical Application of Defensive Techniques

Scenario-Based Training: Practice defensive techniques in realistic scenarios to simulate potential attack situations. Enlist the help of training partners or instructors to create dynamic scenarios and provide feedback on technique execution.

Focus on Timing and Precision: Emphasize timing and precision in executing defensive techniques. Anticipate the attacker's movements, maintain awareness of distance and positioning, and execute techniques with speed and accuracy.

Adaptability and Versatility: Train in a variety of defensive techniques to develop adaptability and versatility in responding to different types of attacks. Incorporate blocks, strikes, joint locks, and escapes into your training regimen to build a well-rounded skillset.

Realistic Stressors: Introduce realistic stressors into training, such as verbal aggression, limited visibility, or multiple attackers, to simulate the adrenaline and pressure of a real-life confrontation. Practice maintaining composure, making quick decisions, and executing techniques effectively under stress.

Key Principles of Effective Defense

Awareness: Stay alert and aware of your surroundings to recognize potential threats and preemptively position yourself for defense.

Distance Management: Maintain a safe distance from potential attackers whenever possible, using footwork and movement to create space or close the distance as needed.

Controlled Response: Respond to threats with controlled and deliberate actions, avoiding panic or excessive force that may escalate the situation.

Escape and Evasion: Prioritize escape and evasion whenever feasible, seeking opportunities to disengage from a confrontation and seek safety.

Continual Training: Regularly practice and refine defensive techniques through ongoing training and skill development to maintain proficiency and readiness.

Effective defensive techniques are essential components of personal safety and self-defense, empowering individuals to protect themselves and others from physical harm. By mastering blocks, strikes, joint locks, and escape techniques, individuals can enhance their ability to respond confidently and effectively to a wide range of attacks and confrontations. Integrating realistic scenario training, focusing on timing and precision, and adhering to key principles of effective defense contribute to developing a well-rounded self-defense skillset. Ultimately, prioritizing personal safety through continual training, awareness, and preparedness strengthens resilience and promotes a safer and more secure environment for all.

CHAPTER 13. USING PEPPER SPRAY AND PERSONAL ALARMS

Pepper spray and personal alarms are valuable tools for enhancing personal safety and self-defense. They provide individuals with non-lethal options for deterring threats, alerting others to emergencies, and creating opportunities for escape. This chapter explores the benefits, proper use, legal considerations, and effectiveness of pepper spray and personal alarms in various safety and self-defense scenarios.

Pepper Spray: A Non-Lethal Defense Option

Pepper spray, also known as OC (Oleoresin Capsicum) spray, is a self-defense tool that contains a concentrated solution derived from chili peppers. It is designed to cause temporary incapacitation and discomfort to an attacker, allowing the user to escape or seek assistance. Pepper spray is available in various formulations, including sprays, gels, and foams, each offering different ranges and dispersal patterns.

Benefits of Pepper Spray:

Non-Lethal: Pepper spray is a non-lethal option for self-defense, causing temporary incapacitation without causing long-term harm or injury.

Effective Deterrent: The intense burning sensation and temporary blindness caused by pepper spray can deter attackers and create opportunities for escape.

Compact and Portable: Pepper spray is compact, lightweight, and easy to carry, making it a convenient self-defense tool for individuals of all ages.

Versatile: Pepper spray can be used in various situations, including outdoor activities, walking or jogging, public transit, and home defense.

Proper Use of Pepper Spray:

Aim for the Eyes and Face: When deploying pepper spray, aim for the attacker's eyes and face to maximize the effects and incapacitate them effectively.

Maintain Distance: Use pepper spray from a safe distance to prevent the attacker from grabbing or disarming you. Most pepper sprays have a recommended range for optimal effectiveness.

Short Bursts: Use short, controlled bursts of pepper spray rather than continuous spraying to conserve the product and ensure proper coverage.

Practice and Familiarity: Familiarize yourself with the operation and deployment of pepper spray through practice drills and training sessions. Ensure quick access and readiness in case of an emergency.

Legal Considerations:

Before purchasing and carrying pepper spray, it is essential to familiarize yourself with local laws and regulations regarding its use. Some key legal considerations include:

Legal Age: Many jurisdictions have a minimum age requirement for purchasing and possessing pepper spray. Ensure compliance with age restrictions to avoid legal repercussions.

Restricted Areas: Some locations, such as schools, government buildings, and airports, may prohibit the possession of pepper spray. Be aware of restricted areas and adhere to relevant regulations.

Use in Self-Defense: Pepper spray should only be used in self-defense situations where there is an imminent threat of harm. Avoid using pepper spray as a form of aggression or retaliation, as this may lead to legal consequences.

Personal Alarms: Enhancing Alertness and Safety

Personal alarms are compact devices designed to emit loud sounds or alerts when activated. They serve as effective tools for drawing attention to emergencies, deterring attackers, and summoning assistance from bystanders or authorities. Personal alarms come in various forms, including keychain alarms, wearable devices, and smartphone apps, offering versatility and convenience for users.

Benefits of Personal Alarms:

Audible Deterrent: The loud sound emitted by personal alarms can startle attackers and draw attention to the situation, increasing the chances of intervention or assistance.

Quick Activation: Personal alarms are designed for quick and easy activation, allowing users to summon help promptly in emergencies.

Discreet and Portable: Personal alarms are often compact, lightweight, and easy to carry, making them ideal for individuals of all ages and lifestyles.

Versatile: Personal alarms can be used in various situations, including outdoor activities, travel, walking alone, and home security.

Proper Use of Personal Alarms:

Accessible Placement: Keep your personal alarm in a readily accessible location, such as a pocket, purse, or keychain, for quick activation in emergencies.

Practice Activation: Familiarize yourself with the operation and activation of your personal alarm through practice drills. Ensure that you can activate the alarm quickly and confidently when needed.

Use in Emergencies: Activate your personal alarm when faced with a threat or emergency situation that requires immediate attention or assistance. The loud sound can attract help and deter potential attackers.

Integration of Pepper Spray and Personal Alarms:

While both pepper spray and personal alarms are effective standalone tools for personal safety, they can also complement each other when used together. Integrating pepper spray and a personal alarm into your self-defense strategy offers a multi-layered approach to safety, providing options for deterring threats, alerting others to emergencies, and increasing your ability to respond effectively to potential dangers.

Training and Preparedness:

To maximize the effectiveness of pepper spray and personal alarms in self-defense scenarios, consider the following training and preparedness tips:

Scenario-Based Training: Practice using pepper spray and activating your personal alarm in realistic scenarios to simulate emergency situations. Enlist the help of a training partner or instructor to create dynamic scenarios and assess your response capabilities.

Awareness and Vigilance: Maintain situational awareness and vigilance in your surroundings to recognize potential threats and take proactive measures for personal safety.

Regular Maintenance: Ensure that your pepper spray and personal alarm are in good working condition by regularly checking expiration dates, battery levels (for alarms), and overall functionality.

Legal Compliance: Adhere to local laws and regulations regarding the possession and use of pepper spray and personal alarms. Familiarize yourself with any restrictions or requirements to avoid legal issues.

Enhancing Personal Safety with Pepper Spray and Personal Alarms

Pepper spray and personal alarms are valuable tools for enhancing personal safety and self-defense, offering non-lethal options for deterring threats, alerting others to emergencies, and creating opportunities for escape. By understanding the benefits, proper use, legal considerations, and integration strategies for pepper spray and personal alarms, individuals can bolster their readiness and confidence in responding to potential dangers. Incorporating these tools into a comprehensive self-defense strategy, along with training, awareness, and preparedness, contributes to a safer and more secure environment for individuals of all ages and backgrounds.

CHAPTER 14. UNDERSTANDING NON-LETHAL WEAPONS

In the realm of personal safety and self-defense, non-lethal weapons play a crucial role in providing individuals with effective tools to deter threats, defend against attacks, and enhance overall safety. This chapter explores various types of non-lethal weapons, their benefits, proper use, legal considerations, and integration into comprehensive self-defense strategies.

What Are Non-Lethal Weapons?

Non-lethal weapons, also known as less-lethal or less-than-lethal weapons, are devices designed to incapacitate, deter, or immobilize targets without causing fatal injuries. Unlike lethal weapons such as firearms or knives, non-lethal weapons are intended to minimize the risk of permanent harm or death while still providing effective means of self-defense. Non-lethal weapons encompass a wide range of devices, including pepper spray, stun guns, batons, tasers, personal alarms, and more.

Benefits of Non-Lethal Weapons:

Reduced Risk of Fatality: Non-lethal weapons are designed to incapacitate or deter threats without causing fatal injuries, reducing the risk of unintended harm or fatalities.

Effective Deterrent: The visible presence or deployment of non-lethal weapons can serve as a deterrent to potential attackers, dissuading them from initiating or continuing hostile actions.

Versatility: Non-lethal weapons come in various forms and functionalities, offering versatility and options for different self-defense scenarios and preferences.

Legal Compliance: Many non-lethal weapons are legal to possess and use in self-defense, provided they are used responsibly and in accordance with applicable laws and regulations.

Types of Non-Lethal Weapons:

Pepper Spray: Pepper spray, also known as OC spray, is a common non-lethal weapon that contains a concentrated solution derived from chili peppers. It causes temporary blindness, intense burning sensations, and respiratory irritation, incapacitating attackers and providing opportunities for escape.

Stun Guns and Tasers: Stun guns and tasers deliver an electric shock to targets, disrupting muscle function and causing temporary incapacitation. They are effective for close-range defense and immobilizing attackers without causing long-term harm.

Batons: Batons, such as expandable batons or tactical batons, are impact weapons used for striking or blocking attacks. They provide users with a defensive tool for warding off assailants and creating distance.

Personal Alarms: Personal alarms emit loud sounds or alerts when activated, drawing attention to emergencies and deterring attackers. They are compact, portable, and easy to carry, making them ideal for individuals of all ages.

Tactical Flashlights: Tactical flashlights with strobe functions can disorient and distract attackers, providing users with a visual deterrent and tactical advantage in low-light conditions.

Rubber Bullets and Bean Bag Rounds: These less-lethal ammunition options are used by law enforcement for crowd control and riot situations, delivering impact without causing fatal injuries.

Proper Use of Non-Lethal Weapons:

Training and Familiarity: Before using non-lethal weapons, undergo training and familiarize yourself with their operation, safety features, and proper deployment techniques. Practice drills and scenarios to develop proficiency and confidence in using these tools effectively.

Target Identification: Clearly identify your target before deploying non-lethal weapons to avoid unintended harm or injury to bystanders. Maintain awareness of your surroundings and assess potential collateral damage risks.

Effective Range and Limitations: Understand the effective range and limitations of non-lethal weapons, such as the reach of pepper spray, the range of stun guns, and the impact force of batons. Use these weapons within their intended parameters for optimal effectiveness.

De-escalation and Escape: Prioritize de-escalation and escape whenever possible, using non-lethal weapons as a last resort in self-defense situations. Create opportunities to disengage from threats and seek safety while maintaining vigilance and awareness.

Legal Compliance: Adhere to local laws and regulations regarding the possession, use, and deployment of non-lethal weapons. Familiarize yourself with any restrictions, licensing requirements, or prohibited areas to avoid legal repercussions.

Integration into Self-Defense Strategies:

Non-lethal weapons can be integrated into comprehensive self-defense strategies to enhance personal safety and preparedness. Consider the following tips for integrating non-lethal weapons effectively:

Assessment of Threat Levels: Assess the threat level and potential risks in different environments to determine the appropriate non-lethal weapons to carry or deploy.

Layered Defense: Implement a layered defense approach by combining non-lethal weapons with other self-defense techniques, such as physical techniques, awareness training, and de-escalation strategies.

Strategic Access: Carry non-lethal weapons in easily accessible locations, such as pockets, belts, or bags, for quick deployment in emergencies. Ensure that you can access and activate these tools efficiently under stress.

Scenario-Based Training: Practice integrating non-lethal weapons into scenario-based training exercises to simulate realistic self-defense situations. Enlist the help of training partners or instructors to assess your response capabilities and refine your tactics.

Continual Assessment and Improvement: Regularly assess and update your non-lethal weapons and self-defense strategies based on feedback, experience, and changing threat environments. Seek ongoing training and skill development to improve readiness and effectiveness.

Legal Considerations:

It is essential to be aware of legal considerations when using non-lethal weapons for self-defense:

Legal Ownership: Ensure that you are legally permitted to own and carry non-lethal weapons in your area. Familiarize yourself with any licensing requirements or restrictions for specific types of non-lethal weapons.

Use in Self-Defense: Non-lethal weapons should only be used in self-defense situations where there is an imminent threat of harm or danger. Avoid using these weapons in a retaliatory or aggressive manner, as this may lead to legal consequences.

Restricted Areas: Be aware of restricted areas or prohibited zones where the possession or use of non-lethal weapons is not permitted. Adhere to signage, regulations, and local ordinances to avoid legal issues.

Non-lethal weapons are valuable tools for enhancing personal safety, self-defense, and preparedness in a variety of situations. By understanding the benefits, proper use, legal considerations, and integration strategies for non-lethal weapons, individuals can bolster their ability to deter threats, defend against attacks, and navigate potential dangers with confidence. Incorporating non-lethal weapons into a comprehensive self-defense strategy, along with training, awareness, and de-escalation techniques, contributes to a safer and more secure environment for individuals of all backgrounds and lifestyles.

CHAPTER 15. SELF-DEFENSE STRATEGIES FOR DIFFERENT ENVIRONMENTS

(e.g., home, work, public spaces)

Self-defense is a dynamic skillset that adapts to various environments and situations. Whether at home, work, or in public spaces, individuals can employ different strategies and techniques to enhance personal safety and effectively respond to potential threats. This chapter explores self-defense strategies tailored to different environments, providing practical insights and recommendations for navigating each setting with confidence and awareness.

1. Self-Defense at Home

Assessment and Preparation:

Conduct a home security assessment to identify potential vulnerabilities, such as weak entry points or inadequate lighting.

Install security measures such as locks, alarms, and motion-sensing lights to deter intruders and enhance home security.

Keep emergency supplies, including a first aid kit, flashlight, and phone, easily accessible in case of emergencies.

Home Invasion Defense:

Create a safe room or designated area where family members can seek refuge during a home invasion.

Establish a communication plan with family members to alert each other in case of emergencies.

Familiarize yourself with self-defense techniques for close-quarters combat, such as striking, blocking, and evasion.

2. Self-Defense in the Workplace

Awareness and Vigilance:

Maintain situational awareness in the workplace, paying attention to unusual behavior or suspicious individuals.

Report any security concerns or safety hazards to appropriate authorities or supervisors.

Participate in workplace safety training programs to learn self-defense techniques and emergency response protocols.

De-Escalation and Conflict Resolution:

Practice de-escalation techniques to defuse tense situations and prevent conflicts from escalating.

Use assertive communication to set boundaries and address potential threats or harassment in the workplace.

Seek support from HR or management if faced with persistent safety concerns or hostile behavior.

3. Self-Defense in Public Spaces

Personal Safety Awareness:

Be mindful of your surroundings in public spaces, including parks, shopping malls, and public transportation.

Avoid distractions such as excessive phone use or wearing headphones that may compromise awareness of potential threats.

Trust your instincts and be cautious of strangers or individuals exhibiting suspicious behavior.

Travel Safety:

Plan travel routes in advance and avoid unfamiliar or high-risk areas, especially at night.

Keep valuables secure and avoid displaying expensive items that may attract unwanted attention.

Use reputable transportation services and share travel itineraries with trusted contacts for added security.

Physical Self-Defense:

Learn basic self-defense techniques, including strikes, blocks, and escapes, to protect yourself in case of physical confrontations.

Carry non-lethal self-defense tools, such as pepper spray or personal alarms, in accordance with local laws and regulations.

Practice situational awareness and assertive behavior to deter potential attackers and create opportunities for escape.

4. Self-Defense in Emergency Situations

Emergency Response Plan:

Develop and review an emergency response plan with family members or colleagues, including evacuation routes and communication protocols.

Establish designated meeting points in case of emergencies to ensure everyone's safety and accountability.

Keep emergency supplies, such as water, food, medications, and first aid kits, readily available in emergency kits or designated areas.

Active Threat Situations:

Follow established emergency procedures, such as lockdowns or evacuations, in response to active threats or violent incidents.

Remain calm and alert, prioritize personal safety and the safety of others, and cooperate with authorities or security personnel.

Avoid confrontation or heroics in active threat situations, and focus on following established protocols and seeking safety.

5. General Self-Defense Tips for All Environments

Maintain Physical Fitness:

Regular exercise and physical fitness contribute to overall strength, agility, and resilience, enhancing your ability to defend yourself if necessary.

Incorporate self-defense training, martial arts, or defensive tactics classes into your fitness regimen to develop practical skills and confidence.

Practice Situational Awareness:

Stay alert and attentive to your surroundings, assessing potential risks and identifying escape routes or safe zones.

Trust your intuition and be proactive in addressing safety concerns or potential threats before they escalate.

Assertive Communication:

Practice assertive communication skills, including setting boundaries, expressing concerns, and asserting your rights confidently and respectfully.

Use assertive language and body posture to convey confidence and deter potential threats or unwanted advances.

Empowering Personal Safety Across Environments

Self-defense strategies tailored to different environments empower individuals to navigate daily life with confidence, awareness, and preparedness. By assessing potential risks, implementing security measures, practicing self-defense techniques, and maintaining vigilance, individuals can enhance personal safety and effectively respond to threats in various settings. Integrating self-defense training, situational awareness, and assertive communication into everyday routines contributes to a safer and more secure environment for individuals, families, and communities as a whole.

CHAPTER 16. CYBER SAFETY AND DIGITAL SECURITY

In today's interconnected world, cyber safety and digital security are paramount for personal safety and well-being. As technology continues to evolve, so do the risks associated with online activities. This chapter delves into essential strategies, best practices, and tools for safeguarding personal information, protecting against cyber threats, and promoting digital security in everyday life.

Understanding Cyber Threats

Cyber threats encompass a wide range of malicious activities aimed at compromising digital security and exploiting vulnerabilities in online systems and networks. Common cyber threats include:

Malware: Malicious software such as viruses, worms, Trojans, and ransomware designed to infect devices, steal data, or disrupt operations.

Phishing: Deceptive emails, messages, or websites designed to trick users into disclosing sensitive information such as passwords, credit card details, or personal data.

Identity Theft: Unauthorized access or use of personal information to impersonate individuals, commit fraud, or gain access to financial accounts.

Social Engineering: Manipulative techniques used to exploit human psychology and trick individuals into divulging confidential information or granting access to sensitive data.

Cyberstalking and Harassment: Persistent online harassment, stalking, or bullying behavior that targets individuals and poses threats to their safety and well-being.

Essential Cyber Safety Practices

Strong Password Management: Use complex, unique passwords for each online account and regularly update them. Consider using password managers to securely store and generate strong passwords.

Two-Factor Authentication (2FA): Enable 2FA for added security on accounts that offer this feature. 2FA requires an additional verification step, such as a text message or authentication app, to access accounts.

Secure Wi-Fi Networks: Use secure, encrypted Wi-Fi networks at home and in public places. Avoid connecting to unsecured or unfamiliar networks that may be compromised.

Regular Software Updates: Keep operating systems, applications, and antivirus software up to date with the latest security patches and updates to protect against vulnerabilities.

Safe Browsing Habits: Exercise caution when clicking on links, downloading attachments, or visiting unfamiliar websites. Be wary of phishing attempts and verify the legitimacy of websites and sources before providing personal information.

Data Backup: Regularly back up important files and data to secure storage locations, such as external hard drives or cloud services. In the event of data loss or ransomware attacks, backups ensure you can recover essential information.

Privacy Settings: Review and adjust privacy settings on social media platforms, devices, and online accounts to control who can access your information and how it is shared.

Cybersecurity Awareness: Stay informed about emerging cyber threats, scams, and security best practices through reputable sources and cybersecurity awareness training programs.

Protecting Personal Information

Secure Online Transactions: Use secure payment methods and websites with HTTPS encryption when making online purchases or entering sensitive financial information.

Limit Data Sharing: Minimize the amount of personal information shared online, especially on social media platforms, public forums, and unsecured websites.

Be Cautious with Personal Details: Avoid sharing sensitive information such as full names, addresses, birthdates, and financial details in public or insecure online settings.

Use Privacy Tools: Utilize privacy-enhancing tools and technologies, such as virtual private networks (VPNs), encrypted messaging apps, and anonymous browsing modes, to protect online activities and communications.

Educate and Empower: Educate family members, colleagues, and peers about cyber safety practices, digital security risks, and strategies for protecting personal information.

Preventing Cyberbullying and Online Harassment

Digital Etiquette: Promote positive digital behavior, respect, and empathy in online interactions. Encourage civil discourse and discourage cyberbullying, harassment, or hate speech.

Report Abuse: Report instances of cyberbullying, harassment, or threatening behavior to appropriate authorities, platforms, or support services. Keep evidence such as screenshots or messages for documentation.

Protecting Children Online: Monitor children's online activities, educate them about online safety, and establish clear guidelines for responsible digital behavior and communication.

Seek Support: Offer support and resources to individuals experiencing cyberbullying or online harassment. Encourage them to seek help from trusted adults, mental health professionals, or support organizations.

Empowering Digital Resilience

Continuous Learning: Stay informed about evolving cyber threats, digital security trends, and best practices through ongoing education and awareness initiatives.

Risk Assessment: Conduct regular risk assessments of digital activities, devices, and online habits to identify potential vulnerabilities and areas for improvement.

Collaborative Approach: Foster collaboration and information sharing among peers, organizations, and communities to address cybersecurity challenges collectively and promote a culture of digital resilience.

Adaptability: Remain adaptable and proactive in responding to emerging cyber threats, implementing security measures, and adjusting strategies as needed to enhance digital safety and security.

Promoting Digital Safety and Security

Cyber safety and digital security are essential components of personal safety and self-defense in today's interconnected world. By understanding common cyber threats, implementing best practices for digital safety, protecting personal information, preventing cyberbullying and online harassment, and empowering digital resilience, individuals can navigate online environments with confidence, awareness, and resilience. Promoting a culture of cybersecurity awareness, education, and collaboration contributes to a safer and more secure digital landscape for individuals, families, businesses, and communities alike.

CHAPTER 17. TRAVEL SAFETY TIPS

Traveling is an exciting and enriching experience, offering opportunities to explore new destinations, cultures, and adventures. However, it's essential to prioritize safety and preparedness while traveling to ensure a smooth and enjoyable journey. This chapter provides comprehensive travel safety tips, including pre-trip planning, on-the-go strategies, and emergency preparedness measures, to help travelers navigate unfamiliar environments with confidence and resilience.

1. Pre-Trip Planning

1.1 Research Destination: Before embarking on your trip, conduct thorough research about your destination. Familiarize yourself with local customs, laws, cultural norms, and potential safety concerns. Understand the political climate, health advisories, and any travel restrictions or warnings issued for the region.

1.2 Secure Travel Documents: Ensure that your travel documents, including passports, visas, identification cards, travel insurance, and itinerary, are up to date and stored securely. Make copies of essential documents and store them separately from the originals in case of loss or theft.

1.3 Share Itinerary: Share your travel itinerary, contact information, and emergency contacts with trusted family members, friends, or colleagues. Provide them with copies of your travel documents and keep them informed of your whereabouts during the trip.

1.4 Health Preparation: Visit a healthcare provider or travel clinic for necessary vaccinations, medications, and health precautions based on your destination. Carry a first aid kit, prescription medications, and health insurance information while traveling.

1.5 Financial Security: Notify your bank or financial institution of your travel plans to avoid any disruptions or fraud alerts on your accounts. Carry multiple forms of payment, including cash, credit cards, and travel money cards, and store them securely.

2. On-the-Go Safety Strategies

2.1 Stay Aware: Maintain situational awareness at all times while traveling. Be observant of your surroundings, avoid distractions such as excessive use of electronic devices, and trust your instincts if something feels off or suspicious.

2.2 Secure Belongings: Keep valuables, including passports, wallets, electronic devices, and cameras, secure and out of sight. Use hotel safes or secure locks for storage, and avoid displaying expensive items in public or unfamiliar environments.

2.3 Use Reliable Transportation: Opt for reputable transportation services, such as licensed taxis, rideshare apps, or public transportation systems with positive reviews and safety ratings. Verify vehicle details, driver credentials, and fares before getting into a vehicle.

2.4 Avoid Isolated Areas: Stay in well-populated, well-lit areas, especially at night. Avoid isolated alleys, deserted streets, or unfamiliar neighborhoods where the risk of crime or harassment may be higher.

2.5 Emergency Communication: Carry a charged mobile phone with emergency contacts programmed and local emergency numbers saved. Familiarize yourself with how to access emergency services, consulate or embassy contacts, and medical facilities in your destination.

3. Emergency Preparedness

3.1 Emergency Contact Information: Keep a list of emergency contacts, including local authorities, embassy or consulate information, travel insurance providers, and medical facilities. Store this information in multiple locations, including your phone, wallet, and hotel room.

3.2 Travel Insurance: Purchase comprehensive travel insurance that covers medical emergencies, trip cancellations, lost or stolen belongings, and emergency evacuations. Familiarize yourself with the coverage details, claims process, and emergency assistance services provided by your insurance provider.

3.3 Communication Plan: Establish a communication plan with travel companions or family members to stay connected during the trip. Agree on meeting points, check-in times, and backup communication methods in case of network disruptions or emergencies.

3.4 Local Laws and Customs: Respect local laws, customs, and cultural sensitivities while traveling. Be mindful of dress codes, photography restrictions, public behavior norms, and alcohol or substance regulations in different countries or regions.

3.5 Emergency Funds: Carry emergency cash or a backup payment method in case of unexpected expenses, transportation disruptions, or emergencies requiring immediate financial assistance. Keep small denominations for convenience and avoid displaying large amounts of money in public.

4. Additional Travel Safety Tips

4.1 Language Basics: Learn essential phrases in the local language, including greetings, directions, emergency phrases, and basic communication skills. Use translation apps or language guides for assistance if needed.

4.2 Cultural Sensitivity: Be respectful and open-minded when interacting with locals and experiencing different cultures. Avoid sensitive topics, gestures, or behaviors that may be offensive or disrespectful.

4.3 Weather Awareness: Stay informed about weather conditions and natural disaster risks in your destination. Prepare for extreme weather events, such as storms, hurricanes, earthquakes, or heatwaves, by following local advisories and safety guidelines.

4.4 Personal Health: Prioritize personal health and well-being during travel. Stay hydrated, get adequate rest, practice good hygiene, and follow recommended safety precautions, such as wearing sunscreen, insect repellent, or protective gear as needed.

4.5 Cultural Experiences: Embrace cultural experiences, try local cuisine, participate in cultural activities, and engage with communities respectfully. Be mindful of sustainable tourism practices, environmental conservation, and responsible travel behaviors.

Safe and Enjoyable Travel

By incorporating these travel safety tips into your trip planning, on-the-go strategies, and emergency preparedness measures, you can enhance your personal safety, confidence, and enjoyment while traveling. Remember to stay informed, remain vigilant, trust your instincts, and prioritize preparation to navigate unfamiliar environments with resilience and peace of mind. Safe travels!

CHAPTER 18. EMERGENCY PREPAREDNESS AND FIRST AID

Emergency situations can occur unexpectedly, and being prepared with the knowledge and skills to respond effectively can make a significant difference in ensuring personal safety and well-being. This chapter delves into essential emergency preparedness measures, first aid techniques, and proactive strategies for managing emergencies in various settings.

1. Understanding Emergency Preparedness

1.1 Risk Assessment: Conduct a risk assessment to identify potential hazards and vulnerabilities in your environment. Consider factors such as natural disasters, medical emergencies, accidents, and security threats that may impact personal safety.

1.2 Emergency Plan: Develop an emergency plan tailored to your needs, location, and potential risks. Include evacuation routes, emergency contacts, communication methods, meeting points, and essential supplies in your plan.

1.3 Emergency Kit: Assemble an emergency kit containing essential items for survival and safety. Items to include may vary but can include water, non-perishable food, first aid supplies, medications, flashlight, batteries, multi-tool, blankets, and important documents.

1.4 Communication: Establish communication protocols with family members, colleagues, or roommates in case of emergencies. Agree on check-in times, emergency contacts, and methods of communication, such as mobile phones, walkie-talkies, or designated meeting points.

1.5 Practice Drills: Conduct regular emergency drills and simulations to practice evacuation procedures, first aid skills, and communication protocols. Familiarize yourself and others with emergency equipment, exits, and safety procedures.

2. First Aid Basics

2.1 Assessing the Situation: When encountering an emergency, assess the situation calmly and quickly. Ensure personal safety first before providing assistance to others. Evaluate the nature and severity of injuries, hazards, or threats present.

2.2 ABCs of First Aid:

Airway: Check the person's airway for obstructions or blockages. Clear the airway if necessary, by tilting the head back and lifting the chin.

Breathing: Assess the person's breathing. Look, listen, and feel for signs of breathing (chest rise and fall, air movement, and sounds).

Circulation: Check for signs of circulation, such as a pulse or color in the skin. Perform CPR if needed and trained to do so.

2.3 Basic First Aid Techniques:

Bleeding Control: Apply direct pressure to wounds to stop bleeding. Use clean dressings or cloth and elevate the injured limb if possible.

Burns: Cool burns with cold water or a cold compress. Cover burns with a clean, non-adhesive bandage and seek medical attention for severe burns.

Fractures: Immobilize fractures or suspected fractures with splints or makeshift supports. Do not move the injured person unless necessary for safety.

Choking: Perform abdominal thrusts (Heimlich maneuver) for conscious choking victims. Encourage coughing and provide assistance as needed.

2.4 CPR and AED Training: Consider undergoing CPR (Cardiopulmonary Resuscitation) and AED (Automated External Defibrillator) training to learn life-saving techniques for cardiac emergencies. CPR involves chest compressions and rescue breaths, while an AED delivers an electrical shock to restore heart rhythm.

2.5 First Aid Kit: Keep a well-stocked first aid kit in accessible locations, such as homes, workplaces, vehicles, and travel bags. Include bandages, gauze, adhesive tape, antiseptic wipes, scissors, tweezers, gloves, pain relievers, and CPR mask.

3. Emergency Response Strategies

3.1 Stay Calm: Maintain a calm and composed demeanor during emergencies to think clearly and make informed decisions. Avoid panicking or rushing into actions that may compromise safety.

3.2 Call for Help: If needed, call emergency services (such as 911 or local equivalents) for professional medical assistance, police intervention, or fire rescue. Provide clear and accurate information about the emergency, location, and number of individuals involved.

3.3 Evacuation Procedures: Follow established evacuation procedures in case of fire, natural disasters, or other emergencies requiring evacuation. Exit the area calmly, assist others if possible, and gather at designated meeting points.

3.4 Communication: Communicate with emergency responders, authorities, or security personnel as needed. Provide updates, follow instructions, and cooperate with professionals to manage the situation effectively.

3.5 Reassure and Support: Offer reassurance and support to individuals affected by emergencies. Provide first aid, comfort, and emotional support while waiting for professional assistance.

4. Personal Safety Considerations

4.1 Protective Gear: Wear appropriate personal protective equipment (PPE) such as gloves, masks, goggles, or helmets when providing first aid or handling hazardous materials. Ensure PPE is clean, properly fitted, and in good condition.

4.2 Scene Safety: Assess the safety of the environment before providing first aid. Ensure there are no ongoing hazards, such as fires, electrical hazards, or unstable structures, that could endanger rescuers or victims.

4.3 Good Samaritan Laws: Familiarize yourself with Good Samaritan laws in your area, which provide legal protection to individuals providing reasonable assistance in emergencies. Understand your rights and responsibilities as a first responder or bystander rendering aid.

4.4 Emotional Resilience: Maintain emotional resilience and seek support if needed after experiencing or witnessing traumatic events. Practice self-care, debriefing, and access mental health resources as necessary.

5. Additional Resources and Training

5.1 First Aid Training: Consider enrolling in certified first aid courses, CPR training, and emergency response programs offered by reputable organizations, healthcare providers, or community centers. Stay updated with refresher courses and practice sessions regularly.

5.2 Emergency Apps: Download emergency preparedness apps or tools that provide information, guidance, and alerts for various emergencies. These apps may include first aid instructions, emergency contacts, disaster preparedness tips, and real-time alerts.

5.3 Community Resources: Connect with local emergency services, fire departments, Red Cross chapters, or community organizations for additional resources, training opportunities, and support networks related to emergency preparedness and first aid.

Empowering Emergency Preparedness and First Aid Skills

By incorporating these emergency preparedness measures, first aid techniques, and proactive strategies into your safety toolkit, you can enhance your ability to respond effectively to emergencies and assist others in need. Remember to stay informed, practice regularly, seek training and resources, and prioritize safety in all aspects of daily life. Empowering yourself with knowledge, skills, and preparedness contributes to a safer and more resilient community for everyone.

CHAPTER 19. BUILDING A PERSONAL SAFETY PLAN

I n today's dynamic and sometimes unpredictable world, having a comprehensive personal safety plan is essential for protecting oneself and responding effectively to potential threats. A personal safety plan encompasses strategies, resources, and proactive measures designed to enhance personal safety, mitigate risks, and promote a sense of security in various situations. This chapter explores the components of building a robust personal safety plan, including risk assessment, preparedness measures, communication strategies, and empowerment techniques.

1. Risk Assessment

1.1 Identify Potential Risks: Begin by identifying potential risks and threats that may affect your personal safety. Consider factors such as your daily activities, environment, travel routines, social interactions, and online presence. Common risks may include physical confrontations, accidents, natural disasters, cyber threats, harassment, or medical emergencies.

1.2 Evaluate Vulnerabilities: Assess your vulnerabilities and areas of concern based on the identified risks. Consider factors such as physical capabilities, health conditions, mobility limitations, familiarity with self-defense techniques, knowledge of emergency procedures, and access to resources or support systems.

1.3 Prioritize Risks: Prioritize risks based on severity, likelihood of occurrence, and potential impact on personal safety. Focus on addressing high-priority risks first while considering preventive measures and contingency plans for lower-priority risks.

2. Preparedness Measures

2.1 Personal Safety Training: Equip yourself with essential personal safety skills, self-defense techniques, and first aid knowledge through certified training programs, workshops, or online courses. Learn how to assess threats, de-escalate confrontations, defend against attacks, and provide basic medical assistance.

2.2 Emergency Kits: Prepare emergency kits tailored to different scenarios, such as home emergencies, travel situations, or outdoor activities. Include essential items such as first aid supplies, water, non-perishable food, flashlights, batteries, multi-tools, emergency blankets, and communication devices.

2.3 Communication Plan: Develop a communication plan with family members, trusted contacts, or support networks to stay connected during emergencies. Share contact information, emergency protocols, meeting points, and alternative communication methods in case of disruptions.

2.4 Information Management: Organize and store important information securely, including personal identification, medical records, emergency contacts, insurance policies, financial information, and legal documents. Keep physical copies and digital backups in safe locations accessible during emergencies.

2.5 Home Security: Enhance home security by implementing measures such as sturdy locks, security systems, motion-sensing lights, surveillance cameras, reinforced doors and windows, and safe rooms or designated shelter areas. Conduct regular home security checks and address vulnerabilities promptly.

3. Communication Strategies

3.1 Emergency Contacts: Maintain a list of emergency contacts, including local authorities, medical services, fire departments, police stations, poison control centers, family members, neighbors, and trusted friends or colleagues. Store contact information in multiple formats, such as phone contacts, written lists, and digital notes.

3.2 Communication Devices: Ensure access to reliable communication devices, such as mobile phones, landlines, two-way radios, or satellite phones, with sufficient battery life, signal strength, and network coverage. Keep chargers, power banks, and backup batteries as part of your communication kit.

3.3 Alert Systems: Subscribe to alert systems, emergency notifications, weather alerts, and community warning systems provided by local authorities, government agencies, or mobile apps. Stay informed about potential threats, evacuation orders, shelter locations, and safety instructions.

3.4 Check-In Procedures: Establish regular check-in procedures with family members, friends, or colleagues when traveling, engaging in outdoor activities, or attending events. Inform them of your itinerary, expected timelines, and methods of communication to ensure accountability and response coordination.

3.5 Safe Words or Signals: Develop safe words or signals with trusted individuals to communicate distress, danger, or the need for assistance discreetly. Use coded messages or gestures that are understood by your support network to initiate help without drawing attention.

4. Empowerment Techniques

4.1 Situational Awareness: Cultivate situational awareness by staying attentive, observant, and alert to your surroundings. Be mindful of potential threats, changes in environment, suspicious behavior, and safety hazards. Trust your instincts and intuition in assessing situations.

4.2 Self-Defense Strategies: Learn and practice self-defense strategies tailored to your capabilities, preferences, and comfort levels. Attend self-defense classes, martial arts training, or workshops to develop physical techniques, assertiveness, and confidence in protecting yourself.

4.3 Assertive Communication: Practice assertive communication skills to set boundaries, express concerns, and assert your rights confidently and respectfully. Use clear, direct language, maintain eye contact, and project a confident demeanor in dealing with potential threats or challenging situations.

4.4 Risk Mitigation: Implement risk mitigation strategies to minimize exposure to potential dangers and vulnerabilities. Avoid high-risk areas, unsafe activities, dangerous behaviors, and interactions with suspicious individuals. Use caution in sharing personal information, online activities, and social media engagement.

4.5 Mental and Emotional Resilience: Build mental and emotional resilience to cope with stress, fear, and uncertainty in emergencies or threatening situations. Practice relaxation techniques, mindfulness, positive coping strategies, and seek support from mental health professionals or support networks as needed.

5. Regular Review and Updates

5.1 Periodic Assessments: Regularly review and update your personal safety plan based on changing circumstances, new risks, experiences, and feedback. Conduct periodic risk assessments, practice drills, and scenario-based simulations to test readiness and identify areas for improvement.

5.2 Training and Skill Development: Continue to enhance your personal safety skills, emergency preparedness knowledge, and self-defense techniques through ongoing training, workshops, refresher courses, and skill-building exercises. Stay informed about evolving threats, technologies, and best practices in personal safety.

5.3 Collaboration and Networking: Collaborate with peers, community groups, neighborhood watch programs, safety organizations, and law enforcement agencies to share resources, information, and best practices related to personal safety and self-defense. Participate in community initiatives, safety campaigns, and awareness programs.

Empowering Personal Safety and Self-Defense

Building a personal safety plan is a proactive and empowering approach to enhancing personal safety, self-defense, and resilience in various situations. By incorporating risk assessment, preparedness measures, communication strategies, empowerment techniques, and regular review into your safety plan, you can navigate daily life with confidence, awareness, and preparedness. Empower yourself with knowledge, skills, and resources to protect yourself, respond effectively to emergencies, and promote a culture of safety and security in your community.

CHAPTER 20. CONTINUING YOUR SAFETY JOURNEY

Training and Resources

Congratulations on completing your journey through the chapters of "Safe and Sound: Handbook for Personal Safety and Self-Defense." As you've explored various aspects of personal safety, self-defense, emergency preparedness, and risk management, you've gained valuable insights, strategies, and skills to enhance your safety and well-being. However, the journey towards personal safety is an ongoing process of learning, growth, and empowerment. In this concluding chapter, we delve into the importance of continuing your safety journey through training, education, and accessing valuable resources.

1. Lifelong Learning in Safety

1.1 Importance of Continuous Training: Safety and self-defense skills require continuous learning and practice to maintain proficiency, adapt to new challenges, and stay updated with emerging threats. Commit to lifelong learning as a cornerstone of your safety journey.

1.2 Skill Enhancement: Participate in advanced training programs, workshops, seminars, and certification courses to enhance your personal safety skills, self-defense techniques, emergency response capabilities, and risk assessment expertise.

1.3 Specialized Training: Consider specialized training in areas such as martial arts, firearms safety, wilderness survival, cybersecurity, first aid, crisis intervention, conflict resolution, and situational awareness to broaden your safety toolkit.

1.4 Professional Development: Explore opportunities for professional development in safety-related fields, including security management, risk assessment, emergency planning, law enforcement, healthcare, counseling, and community safety initiatives.

2. Accessing Valuable Resources

2.1 Safety Organizations: Connect with reputable safety organizations, advocacy groups, non-profit organizations, and government agencies dedicated to promoting personal safety, self-defense education, victim support services, and community resilience.

2.2 Online Platforms: Utilize online platforms, forums, social media groups, and digital communities focused on personal safety, self-defense, emergency preparedness, and risk management. Engage in discussions, share experiences, and access valuable resources and insights from experts and peers.

2.3 Safety Apps and Tools: Explore safety apps, mobile tools, and digital resources designed to enhance personal safety, provide emergency alerts, offer self-defense tutorials, facilitate communication, and access resources during crises or threatening situations.

2.4 Educational Materials: Read books, articles, research papers, and educational materials related to personal safety, self-defense tactics, emergency planning, risk assessment methodologies, conflict resolution strategies, and psychological resilience.

3. Empowerment through Networking

3.1 Community Engagement: Engage with your local community, neighborhood watch programs, safety committees, volunteer organizations, and civic groups involved in promoting safety awareness, crime prevention, and community resilience initiatives.

3.2 Networking Opportunities: Attend safety conferences, workshops, seminars, and networking events to connect with safety professionals, industry experts, law enforcement officials, emergency responders, healthcare professionals, and advocates for personal safety and self-defense.

3.3 Peer Support: Seek peer support networks, support groups, mentorship programs, and online communities where individuals share experiences, exchange advice, offer encouragement, and collaborate on safety initiatives.

4. Embracing a Culture of Safety

4.1 Promoting Safety Awareness: Take an active role in promoting safety awareness, education, and advocacy within your social circles, workplace, schools, and communities. Share safety tips, resources, and best practices with others to empower collective safety efforts.

4.2 Teaching and Mentoring: Consider opportunities to teach safety workshops, self-defense classes, first aid training, or safety seminars to empower others with essential skills, knowledge, and confidence in personal safety and self-defense.

4.3 Advocacy and Policy: Advocate for policies, regulations, and initiatives that promote safety, prevent violence, address systemic issues, and support survivors of trauma, abuse, or discrimination. Collaborate with policymakers, community leaders, and advocacy groups to create positive change.

5. Personal Commitment to Safety

5.1 Mindset and Attitude: Maintain a proactive mindset, positive attitude, and commitment to personal safety, well-being, and empowerment. Cultivate resilience, adaptability, and assertiveness in navigating challenges and unexpected situations.

5.2 Risk Assessment and Planning: Continuously assess risks, vulnerabilities, and safety concerns in your environment. Update your safety plan, emergency protocols, communication strategies, and preparedness measures based on changing circumstances and experiences.

5.3 Self-Care and Wellness: Prioritize self-care, mental wellness, and physical health as integral components of personal safety and resilience. Practice stress management techniques, seek support when needed, and foster a balanced lifestyle that supports overall well-being.

Conclusion: Empowered and Prepared

As you continue your safety journey beyond the pages of this handbook, remember that empowerment, preparedness, and education are your strongest allies. By committing to continuous learning, accessing valuable resources, networking with like-minded individuals, and embracing a culture of safety, you empower yourself and contribute to creating safer, more resilient communities.

Your journey doesn't end here—it evolves and grows with each step you take towards personal safety, self-defense proficiency, and holistic well-being. Stay proactive, stay informed, and stay empowered as you navigate life's adventures with confidence, awareness, and resilience.

Thank you for embarking on this journey with "Safe and Sound: Handbook for Personal Safety and Self-Defense." May your path be safe, sound, and filled with empowerment.

Milton Keynes UK
Ingram Content Group UK Ltd.
UKHW052233090424
440866UK00011B/247